Technology Inspired by ANIMALS

I0643969

INVENTIONS INSPIRED BY OCEANIC ANIMALS

Contents

Technology Inspired by ANIMALS

INVENTIONS INSPIRED BY OCEANIC ANIMALS

Tessa Miller and Madeline Nixon

AV2
www.av2books.com

Step 1
Go to **www.av2books.com**

Step 2
Enter this unique code
LYUMPY3BD

Step 3
Explore your interactive eBook!

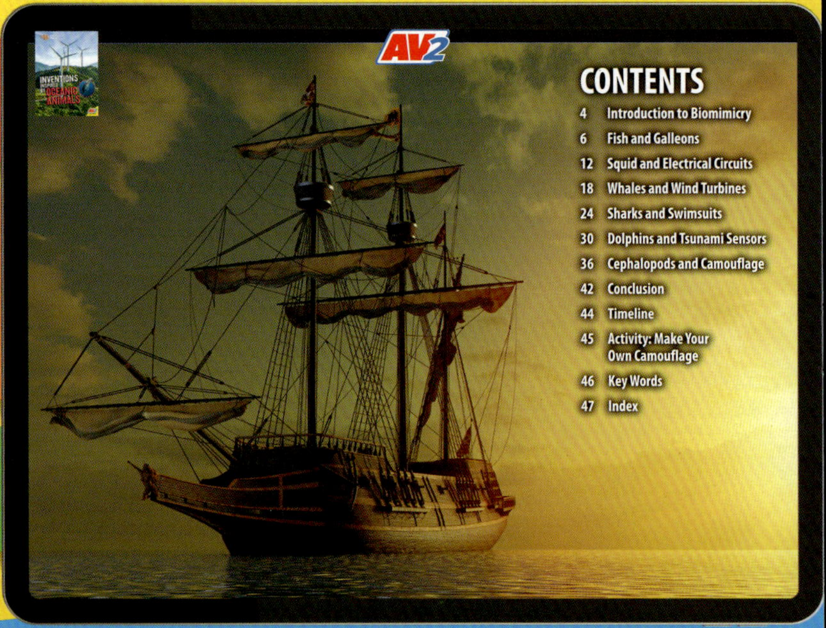

AV2 is optimized for use on any device

Your interactive eBook comes with...

Contents
Browse a live contents page to easily navigate through resources

Audio
Listen to sections of the book read aloud

Videos
Watch informative video clips

Weblinks
Gain additional information for research

Try This!
Complete activities and hands-on experiments

Key Words
Study vocabulary, and complete a matching word activity

Quizzes
Test your knowledge

Slideshows
View images and captions

... and much, much more!

View new titles and product videos at **www.av2books.com**

Introduction to Biomimicry

Earth's oceans are full of mysteries. Scientists think that 95 percent of Earth's oceans are unexplored. New animals and plants are discovered every day. Some ocean animals are as small as a grain of sand. Others are the largest animals on the planet. Many sea creatures have special abilities. These abilities help them survive and thrive deep underwater. People can learn many things by studying these animals.

Nature often gives scientists and **engineers** new ideas. They can use these ideas to help solve problems and make **technology** better. This is called biomimicry. "Bio" means life. "Mimicry" means to copy something else. People have been mimicking underwater animals for hundreds of years. They still do today. From 16th-century ships to the military uniforms of the future, many fascinating technologies have been **inspired** by animals.

Mackerel are a type of fish that live in the ocean and travel in schools. A single school can have thousands of fish and stretch for miles.

Fish and Galleons

Many hundreds of years ago, people did not have advanced technology for travel. They could not drive a car or fly in an airplane. However, they could take a sailing ship. In the 14th and 15th centuries, these ships were slow. It took months for a large sailing ship, such as a carrack, to cross the Atlantic Ocean. A round trip from Spain to the Bahamas could take up to 16 months on a carrack.

These ships were slow because they were huge and heavy. The bodies of the ships were wide and deep. They could carry a large amount of **cargo**, but because they were so slow, they became targets for pirates. They also could not transport food items that might go bad, because trips took too long.

In the 1500s, it took a crew of more than 80 people to sail a galleon.

By the 1500s, people wanted to cross the Atlantic Ocean faster. Shipmakers were working hard to make better ships. They had to come up with a better **design**. In the end, they were inspired by fast-swimming fish from the ocean. This inspiration led to a fast-moving sailing ship—the galleon.

Lessons from Nature

Shipmakers in England studied the body shapes of different fish. One fish they focused on was the mackerel. Mackerel can swim very fast. They are also able to move very precisely. Their bodies are shaped like a teardrop or a torpedo. They have a large, round head and body with a slender tail. Shipmakers realized this shape might work well for ships, too. They started to design a new ship. The body of the ship, called the hull, was shaped more like a mackerel. The shipmakers also looked at fish that swim in **reefs**. These fish have pointed noses. Shipmakers gave the ship a pointed front, called the prow.

Now shipmakers had a ship that was long, narrow, and very fast, like a mackerel. Its pointed prow let it cut through the water smoothly. They called this new ship the *galleon*, which means "little ship" or "armed ship."

Mackerel are very nutritious. They are an important food source for people around the world.

The British galleon's new design made it the fastest ship in the world. Because it was so light and fast, it was used as a guard for slower cargo ships. This saved cargo ships from being attacked by pirates. In the late 1500s, the galleon was used to carry cargo. It could make a round trip from Europe to South America very quickly. Because of the faster travel time, fruits and vegetables could be shipped across longer distances. Many people in Europe were able to buy produce, such as tomatoes, for the first time.

The galleon was important during the Age of Discovery (about 1450–1650). This was a time of world exploration and, sometimes, war.

Mackerels can swim up to **6.8 miles (10.9 kilometers)** per hour. Olympic swimmer Michael Phelps's fastest swim was **6 miles (9.7 km)** per hour.

Tech in Action

The mackerel's unique body inspired a better design for 16th-century battleships.

FINS

Fins are on all sides of a mackerel's body. This allows the fish to move and turn quickly and easily.

SAILS

The galleon's many sails helped it to out-maneuver other ships in battle.

NOSE
A pointed nose helps the fish speed through water.

PROW
The galleon's pointed prow let it cut through air and water.

BODY SHAPE
Mackerels have slim bodies and a torpedo shape. They can swim very quickly in short bursts.

HULL SHAPE
Galleons were long and narrow. They were shaped more like a fish than other ships during that time.

Squid have very complex eyes and brains. This makes them good hunters.

Squid and Electric Circuits

Every day, people depend on indicator lights. These lights show, or indicate, that tools and machines are working. Indicator lights tell people if a battery is charged. But what if the light does not work? What if a battery is dead, but the light does not respond? What if the light just flickers?

This can happen for two reasons. The first is that the electric signal is too slow. Because of this, the light will not turn on or off when it is supposed to. The second is that there is too much **noise**.

Electricity is a type of energy. Technology directs the flow of energy so it can be used to do work.

This makes the electricity bounce back and forth, which causes the light to flicker. These issues can cause big problems for people who need machines to do their jobs, such as doctors.

Otto H. Schmitt was worried about failing indicator lights. In the 1930s, Schmitt was a student. He was studying electrical **circuits**. He hoped to design a new part for circuits. He wanted it to act as a better on/off switch. First, he needed to find an electrical system with a good on/off switch. Then, he could copy how it worked. So Schmitt started looking at nature. What he found was an animal with a complex electrical system in its body—the squid.

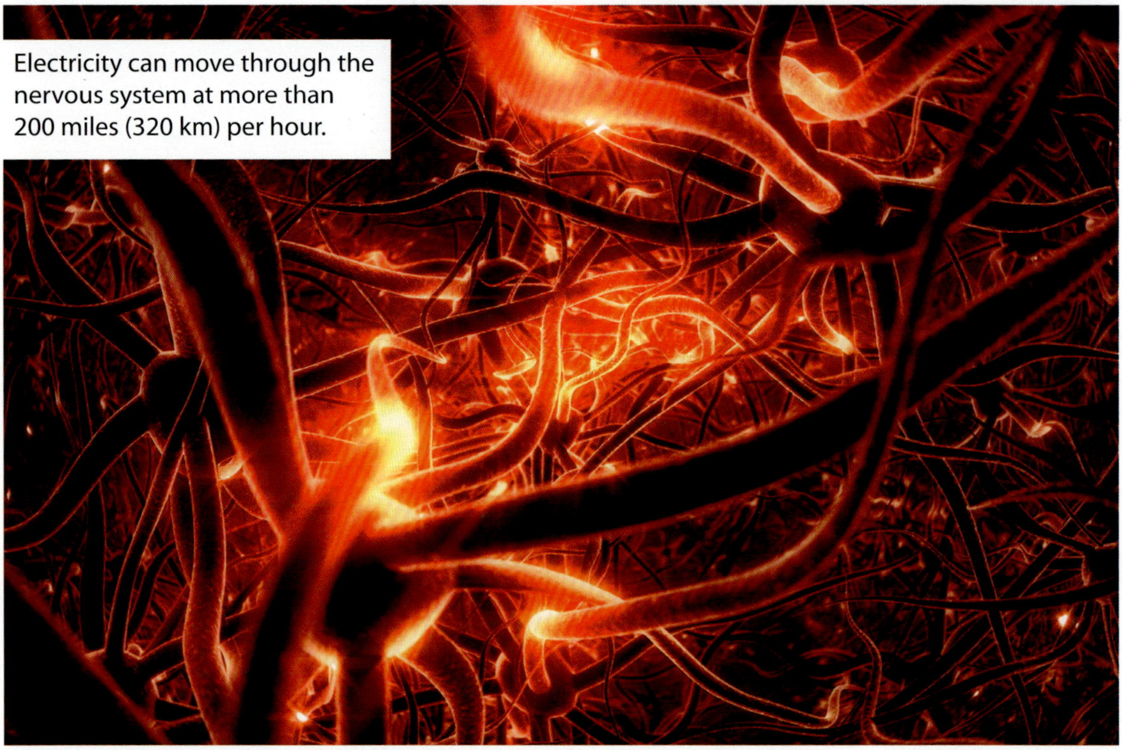

Electricity can move through the nervous system at more than 200 miles (320 km) per hour.

Lessons from Nature

Many animals have a complex **nervous system**. One part of the nervous system is the axon. Axons are like threads or cables. They carry electrical signals around the body. Axons act as an on/off switch for the signals. In squid, axons are really big. They are also very strong. This lets scientists study them easily.

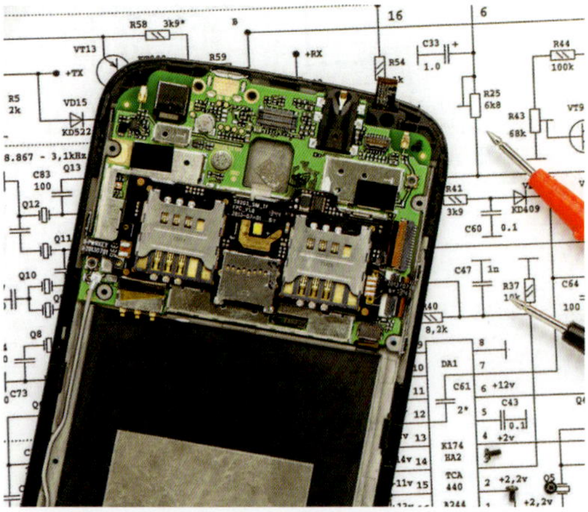

Every cell phone contains a circuit. The circuit powers all of the phone's functions.

Nervous systems can have the same problems as indicator lights. Electrical signals may move too slowly, or there may be too much noise. To solve these problems, squid axons set **thresholds**. First, the squid's brain sends a signal to a tentacle. The signal is a message for the tentacle to move. The signal travels through the axon. The electricity builds up. Then, it crosses the threshold. Like an on/off switch, this **triggers** a response. The tentacle moves.

The Schmitt trigger cannot be affected by noise or current changes.

Schmitt studied squid axons. He saw how their thresholds work. Then, he invented a new part for electrical circuits. It is called the Schmitt trigger. It works just like a squid axon. It sets new thresholds. This turns electricity on and off at the right time. It also reduces noise. Today, the Schmitt trigger is used in millions of machines and electronics, including computers.

There may be more than 500 species of squid in the ocean.

People sometimes mistake squid for octopuses. Squid have **triangle-shaped heads with two fins.** Octopuses have **round heads with fins.**

Tech in Action

Otto Schmitt's study of the squid led to technology many people use every day.

SOLUTION

Squid axons make good on/off switches and control noise. This lets a squid's body respond to messages from the brain quickly.

IMPROVEMENT

Schmitt triggers improve circuits. They reduce noise and act as on/off switches for important electrical signals.

NERVOUS SYSTEM

The squid's nervous system controls electricity in the body.

ELECTRICAL SYSTEM

Cables, circuits, and wires carry electricity around a computer.

THRESHOLD

When energy in a squid axon crosses a threshold, it causes a reaction. This includes movement.

TRIGGER

Schmitt triggers set new thresholds for electrical signals. Electricity has to cross the threshold. This triggers a reaction.

A humpback whale has to eat thousands of pounds of food a day. This gives it the energy it needs to survive.

Whales and Wind Turbines

A weak wind begins to blow. It crosses fields and hills, gaining strength. It was once a small gust. Now it is as fast as a train. Then, it reaches a wind farm. It blows through the towering white wind turbines. The blades of the wind turbines turn, harnessing the power of the wind and turning it into electricity.

This electricity is used to power homes and buildings. Right now, about 6.6 percent of the electricity used in the United States comes from wind power. Scientists want to raise this to 20 percent by 2030. To do this, they have to make windmills more **effective**.

Wind turbines capture wind power and turn it into electricity. A single wind turbine can power about 500 homes.

The answer may have been found—not in the air, but in the water. A scientist named Frank Fish discovered that the flippers of humpback whales work like the blades of wind turbines. But the flippers have bumps called tubercles. They help humpback whales use their flippers more effectively.

The humpback whale has tubercles along its two front fins. It also has them on its forehead, snout, and chin.

Lessons from Nature

To turn in tight circles, whales point their fins straight down. Swimming like this creates whirlpools along the flippers. This creates **drag**, which slows the whale down. Many large whales have tubercles. Tubercles allow water to flow over the flipper. This breaks up whirlpools before they even start. No whirlpools around the fins means less drag. Now, the whale can swim smoothly. Without tubercles, large whales would not be able to turn sharply enough to hunt for fish.

Frank Fish discovered that tubercles work just as well in the air. Engineers are now putting them on fan blades. They can be used for small fans in homes and businesses. They can also be used for wind turbines. Tubercles on the blades help

them spin in less wind. This makes them more efficient. The blades can be built smaller. Those blades are still just as powerful as larger blades. This saves money. It also means wind turbines can be put in more places, including cities.

A typical wind turbine blade is about 10 times the length of a humpback whale fin.

When hunting, a humpback whale **swims in tight circles** around a school of fish. The whale blows **lots of tiny bubbles**. The bubbles **create a net** that catches the fish. The whale then swallows them **in one gulp**.

Tech in Action

Tubercles help a humpback whale move better in the water. They also help a turbine blade move better in the air.

TUBERCLES
Flippers have tubercles on their front edges. These reduce drag.

RIDGES
New blades have ridges cut into the front side. These increase efficiency.

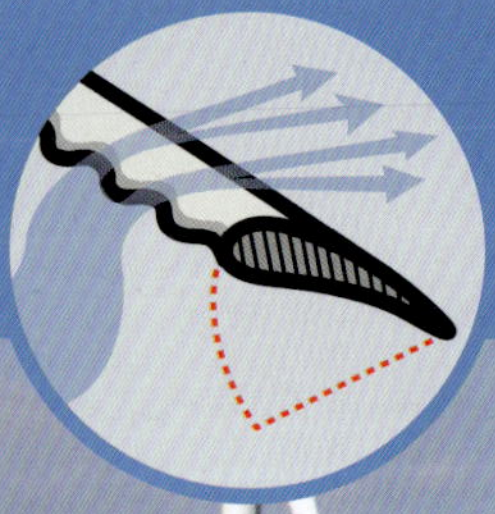

GLIDING

Flippers are shaped like bird wings. The shape helps them glide through the water.

CUTTING

A fan blade has a wing-like shape. This helps it cut through the air more smoothly.

SIZE

Humpback whale flippers are really big. They move through a lot of water.

LENGTH

Wind turbine blades can be as long as a Boeing 747 plane. They move through a lot of air.

Great white sharks never stop swimming. It is part of how they breathe.

Sharks and Swimsuits

The whistle blows. A line of swimmers dives into the water. One swimmer is wearing a shiny gray swimsuit. Stroke for stroke, each swimmer is a powerful **competitor**. They are equally matched. Yet the swimmer in the gray suit is pulling ahead. She reaches the last lap. Finally, she taps the wall. She finished seconds before the next swimmer. She has won the Olympic gold medal.

It is not unusual for Olympic swimmers to swim for two or three hours every day.

What is so special about her suit? Did it give her an edge over her competitors? Her suit was designed to work like a shark's skin. Much like a shark's skin, her suit helped her swim faster.

Sharks are the top **predators** of the oceans. To catch everything they need to eat, they have to be fast. A shark can swim 10 times faster than any human on record. Designers at the swimsuit company Speedo were looking to improve their swimsuits. It makes sense that they looked at sharks to design a new fabric.

Shark scales are not like fish scales. They are actually more like little teeth.

Lessons from Nature

A shark's skin is unique. Each scale is shaped like a fang. It is rounded in the front and pointed in the back. These tiny ridges are called denticles. The denticles lie like feathers on wings. They overlap each other by a little bit. It is just enough to create a surface that bends and moves easily with the shark's movements.

The denticles act like tubercles on whale flippers. Whirlpools might form along a shark's body. Denticles break them up as the shark swims. This creates less drag. Less drag means a shark can swim quickly and smoothly.

Speedo's most popular shark-inspired swimsuits cost at least $300.

Researchers at Speedo used these facts to make a new type of swimsuit. They called it Fastskin. Fastskin fabric is tight but flexible. It has denticles on the surface. The Fastskin swimsuit reduces drag by up to 4 percent. This is a lot during a competition, when every second counts.

Engineers are also looking at shark skin. They are designing a material to coat the outside of planes and ships. Planes would be more **aerodynamic**. Ships would be more **hydrodynamic**. The special coating could save companies a lot of fuel. This would save money and help reduce pollution.

Fastskin swimsuits were not allowed after the **2008 Summer Olympics**. Officials thought they gave swimmers an unfair edge over their competitors.

Tech in Action

Sharks are mighty predators of the deep. People have designed suits so they can swim more like sharks.

SHAPE
Most have long, slim bodies and pointed noses. This shape makes them very hydrodynamic.

FORM
The swimsuit is full length and stiff. This keeps a swimmer's shape long and slim.

DENTICLES

The denticles on a shark's skin reduce its drag.

FABRIC

The Fastskin swimsuit is covered in shark-like denticles.

COVERING

Denticles cover every inch of a shark's body. They make the shark's skin more flexible.

FIT

The special fabric of the Fastskin suit makes the suit more flexible, so it molds to a swimmer's body.

Dolphins and other large sea creatures move to deep water when there is a storm.

Dolphins and Tsunami Sensors

An earthquake rumbles deep out in the ocean. Nobody is around to feel it. But the **tsunami** the quake produces will soon slam into land, destroying everything in its path.

Scientists are working on ways to better **detect** and predict these earthquakes and tsunamis. There are hundreds of tsunami sensors all over Earth's oceans. They are connected to buoys. Buoys are brightly colored objects that float and mark areas of water. Some buoys mark unsafe waters, but not all. And that is not what these buoys are doing.

Underwater sensors can help scientists predict dangerous weather conditions.

When there is an earthquake, a signal is sent from the sensor to a computer on the buoy. The signal goes to a **satellite**. Then it goes to a computer on land. Scientists then study the signal. All this takes a long time. Sometimes a signal is too confusing to figure out.

Scientists want to improve this technology. They are studying how dolphins **communicate**. Dolphins are able to send many sounds through the water. The sounds can travel long distances very quickly.

Lessons from Nature

Dolphins have a special way of communicating. They use many different chirps, tweets, and clicks. Dolphins send these sounds out at multiple **frequencies**. It is like playing one song on several radio stations at once. Sometimes a radio station gets a lot of static. You can always tune into another to keep listening to the song. The ocean is a noisy place. Dolphins cannot always hear each other on a noisy frequency. If this happens, they listen to a different one. This lets dolphins talk without being interrupted. They can even communicate when the water gets rough and choppy.

Dolphins also blow bubbles, move their jaws, and touch fins to communicate.

For eight years, a team of researchers at EvoLogics in Germany studied dolphins. They wanted to see if they could mimic how dolphins communicate. They built a new sensor that uses dolphin-like sounds. When there is an earthquake, it sends signals across many frequencies. The sensor is now being tested in the Indian Ocean. The new technology seems to be giving off much clearer signals. It can let scientists predict natural events, such as tsunamis, sooner. This would give people more time to evacuate and save countless lives each year.

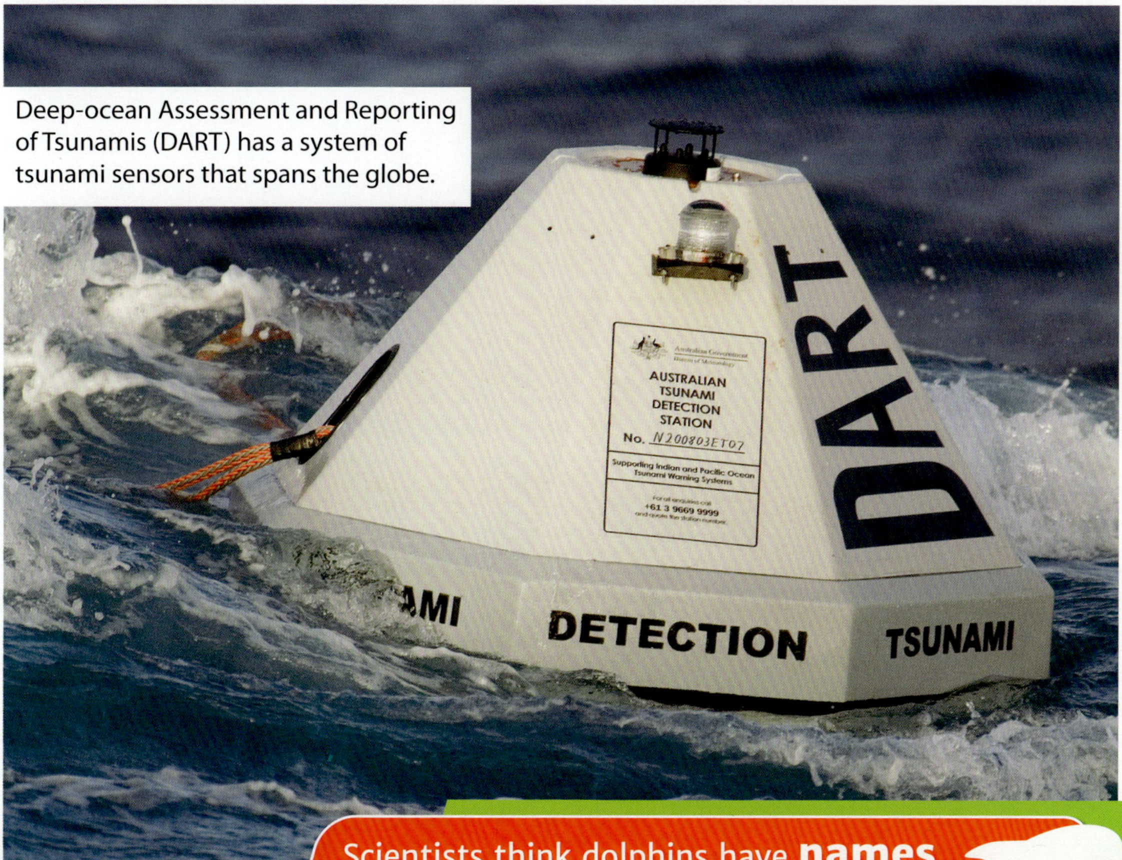

Deep-ocean Assessment and Reporting of Tsunamis (DART) has a system of tsunami sensors that spans the globe.

Scientists think dolphins have **names for each other**. Each dolphin has a **special whistle** that other dolphins use to get its attention.

Tech in Action

By mimicking dolphin calls, people are improving tsunami warning systems in multiple ways.

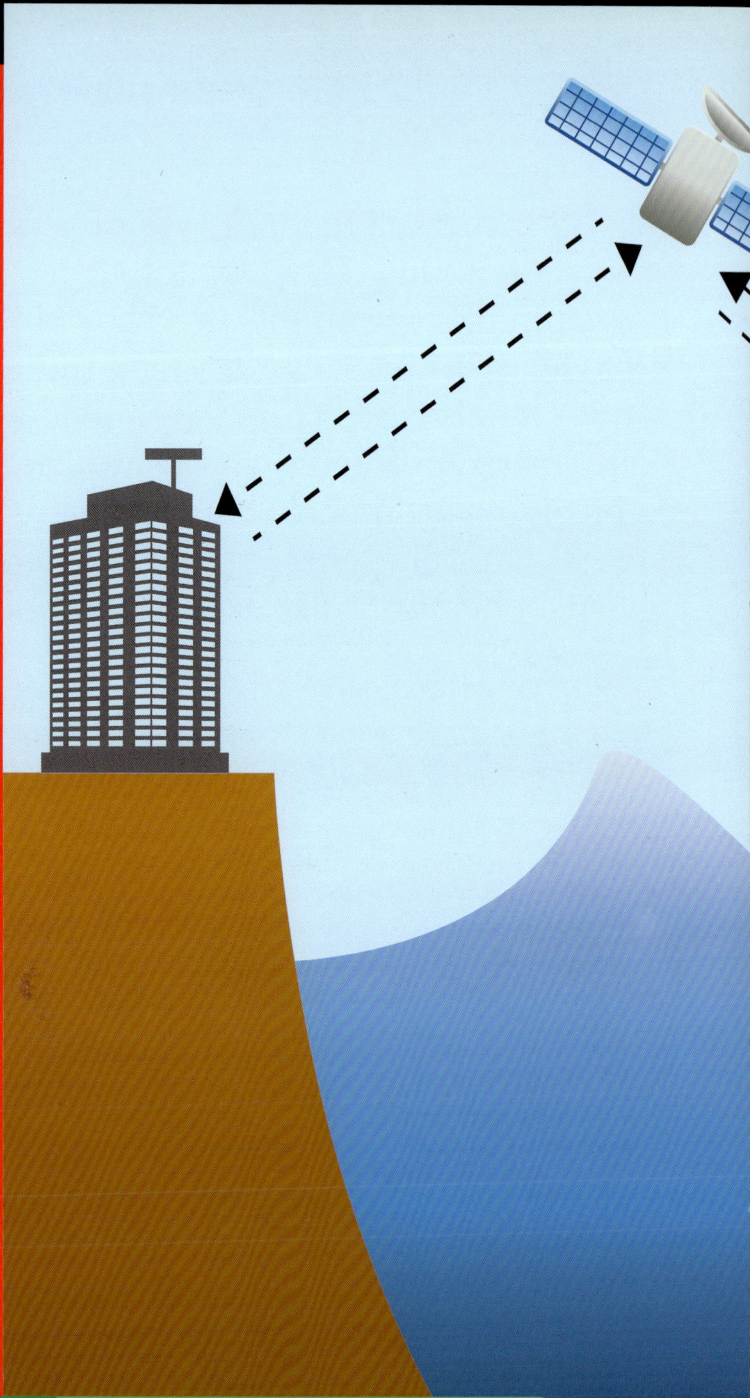

CLEAR

Even in rough seas, dolphin calls are not confused with other sounds.

UNDERSTANDABLE

The new signals are clear and easy for scientists to understand.

CHATTER
Dolphins use chirps, tweets, and clicks to talk to each other.

NOISES
New sonar systems use a range of frequencies to send signals and communicate with satellites.

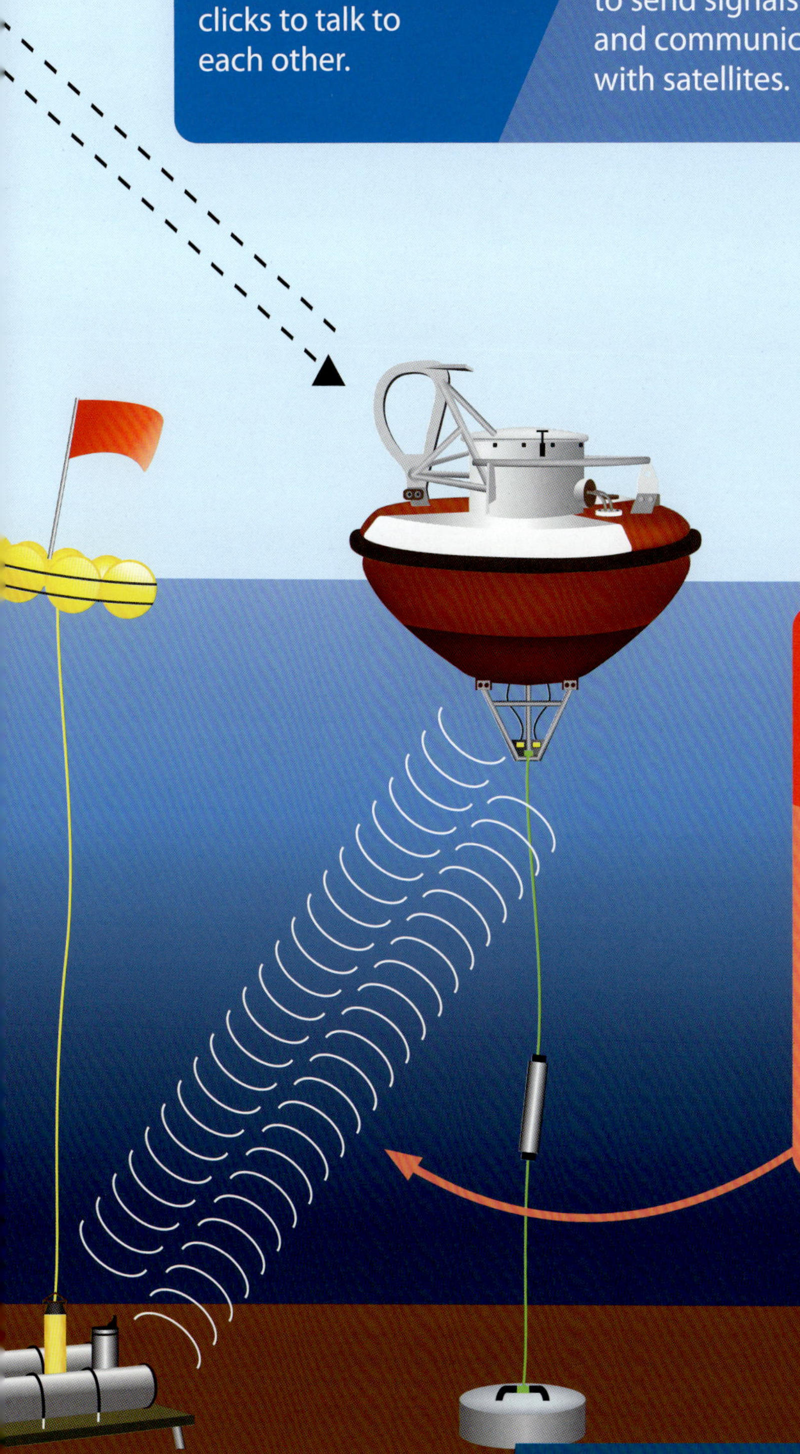

DISTANCE
Dolphin calls travel up to 15.5 miles (25 km) underwater.

RANGE
Signals travel through 11 miles (18 km) of water from the ocean floor.

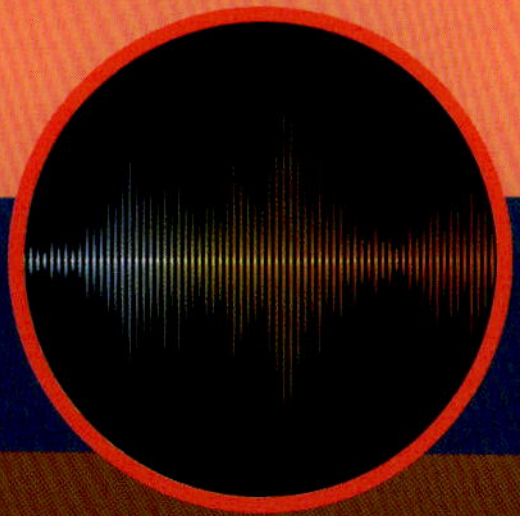

Cephalopods, such as octopuses, have no bones. They can lie very flat. They can also fit through tiny spaces.

Cephalopods and Camouflage

An orange-and-red octopus swims through calm waters. Settling on the sandy bottom, it stretches out eight limbs. Each one digs in the sand, looking for food. Just as a tentacle grasps a clam, the octopus freezes. It looks up. There is a dark shape moving through the water. Slowly, the octopus pulls its limbs back. The color of its skin begins to change. Now, it matches the brown and gray of the sand and rocks around it. The dark shape, a seal, passes over. **Camouflage** has saved the octopus from becoming dinner.

To survive, cephalopods have to be sneaky. These are ocean animals with large heads and long arms. They include octopus, squid, and cuttlefish. Many cephalopods have a special trick. They can change color. They can then match their **environment**. This lets them hide wherever they want. Camouflage lets cephalopods blend into rocks or coral. Other animals use camouflage, too. Green insects can look like leaves. Fish can look like sand on the ocean floor. However, only certain animals can change their colors as they move.

Camouflage may look strange from up close. But from far away, it blends in with rocks, shadows, and plants.

Lessons from Nature

Cephalopods have three layers of skin. Each layer of skin has different color **pigments**. Beneath the skin is a layer of muscle. The muscles act as a trigger. This changes the colors in the skin layers.

Researchers across the United States are working together to create a new type of fabric. This fabric changes colors much like a cephalopod's skin. So far, researchers have been able to make a three-layer fabric. It can change from black to white. The first layer is made up of tiny light sensors. The next layer has small motors. The last layer is made up of color **capsules**. First, the sensors read a color change in the surrounding environment. Then, the motors turn on. They trigger the color capsules. The capsules then change from black to white. This is an important first step in making color-changing fabric.

Cuttlefish use camouflage to hide from predators, such as dolphins. Cuttlefish might also change their colors to communicate.

Scientists are now working to improve this technology. They want to make fabric that can change to any color. The military could use the fabric to design a set of camouflage for every soldier. Car designers want to use it for car paints. In an emergency, ambulances and police cars could change to brighter colors. This would make them more visible to other drivers.

Camouflage protects soldiers and their equipment from enemies.

During **World War I (1914–1918),** some ships were painted with **zebra stripes.** This type of camouflage **breaks up the zebra's outline**, hiding it from predators. In the same way, the stripes **helped hide ships from enemies**.

Tech in Action

Many animals use color-changing camouflage. Soon humans will, too, thanks to biomimicry.

MUSCLES
Muscles trigger the colors to change.

MOTORS
Tiny motors trigger color capsules to change colors.

COLOR CHANGING

Cephalopods have three layers of color-changing skin.

COLOR SWITCHING

Scientists have designed a fabric that changes from black to white.

IN USE

Cephalopods change colors to match their environment. They can hide in plain sight.

FUTURE USE

One day, the fabric may be used for military uniforms. Uniforms would change color as soldiers move through different environments.

Biomimicry of whales has also led to a new water filter. It mimics how humpback and blue whales filter-feed.

Conclusion

There are hundreds of thousands of different types of creatures in the oceans. Many more are waiting to be discovered. Scientists look to the ocean every day for inspiration. This inspiration leads technology in new directions.

For a long time, people did not realize just how intelligent dolphins are. Now, researchers have studied how they communicate. Scientists have mimicked dolphin chirps and clicks to build better tsunami sensors. **Biologists** continue to study dolphin communication. They hope to someday use these chirps and clicks to have conversations with dolphins.

The British Royal Navy is using biomimicry. Designs for future ships have been inspired by underwater animals.

In the past, galleons were made faster because of biomimicry. Shipbuilders copied fish. Now, shipbuilders are designing new submarines. The submarines do not use propellers to move forward. They have flippers and fins to move like whales.

People continue to look deep into the oceans for inspiration. You never know what will be found next.

Timeline

Biomimicry has inspired scientists to create inventions they never would have thought of alone. Oceanic animals have inspired many important inventions.

2003 A company called Sharklet begins creating plastic wrap and catheters inspired by sharkskin to lower risk of infections in hospitals. Sharkskin is one of the cleanest things in the ocean. Unlike other fish, sharks do not grow algae, barnacles, or bacteria.

2005 Mercedes-Benz designs a streamlined car that emits less emissions. Their inspiration for the car came from the yellow boxfish.

2010 Scientists begin to create iron-like military uniforms inspired by sea snails' shells. These shells are strong, armored, and lightweight, protecting sea snails from predators.

2011 Architect Vincent Callebaut designs a sustainable, eco-friendly building capable of housing 1,000 people to help the victims of the 2010 earthquake in Haiti. The building is inspired by coral reefs.

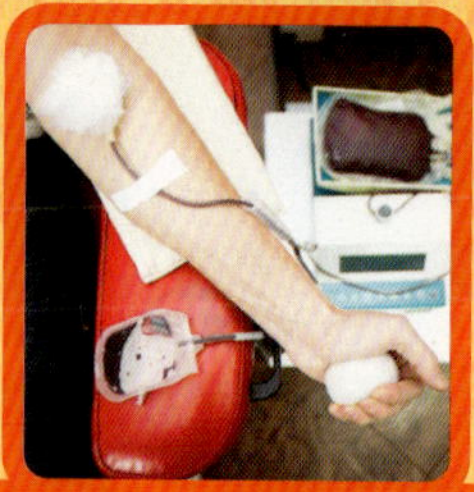

2014 Researchers at the University of Warwick study arctic cod and discover that the fish keep from freezing because they have antifreeze proteins in their blood. This discovery allows them to create a preserve that will help store donated blood longer.

2019 Researchers at Northwestern Engineering and the University of California study sea urchins to create self-sharpening tools. Sea urchins can self-sharpen their spines so that they never dull.

Activity

Make Your Own Camouflage

Have you ever wondered how animals can hide in plain sight? Many do it with camouflage. With this activity, you can design your own camouflage shirt to wear.

What You Need

- Large T-shirt
- Fabric markers and/or paints
- Fabric glue
- Scissors
- Scraps of natural-colored materials, such as streamers, crepe paper, newsprint, tissue paper, etc.
- Paper and pencils

What to Do

1. Break into groups. Assign each group a specific area to blend into. The area can be grass, trees, bushes, rocks, or dirt.
2. With your group, look closely at your environment. Make a list of all the colors, shapes, and textures you see.
3. Sketch out what you want your shirt to look like. Check your list of colors, shapes, and textures.
4. Build your camouflage shirt. Cut shapes out of the natural-colored materials. Glue them to the shirt. You can also use fabric markers and paints to mimic the colors and shapes in your environment.
5. Once the shirt is done (and has dried if paints were used), try it out. Have one group member put it on. Have this person hide in his or her environment. The other groups can then try to find your camouflaged group member.
6. Afterward, think about what made it hard to find people. What made it easy to find them? What would you change to make your camouflage shirt better?

Key Words

aerodynamic: able to move easily through air

biologists: scientists who study living things, such as plants and animals

camouflage: a way of hiding by blending in with your surroundings

capsules: small containers, usually round or cylindrical

cargo: items for sale that are moved by a ship, plane, or truck

circuits: pieces of technology that contain or direct a flow of electricity

communicate: to say or tell; to give information

competitor: someone who takes part in a sport or other pursuit to try to win

design: to make a plan by thinking about the purpose or use of something

detect: to notice something that is hard to see or hear

drag: the force of water or air that pushes against something as it moves

effective: successful in achieving a desired effect or result

engineers: people who plan and build tools, machines, or structures

environment: the air, water, plants, animals, weather, and other things in an area

frequencies: the rates at which vibrations occur, such as the vibration of sound waves

hydrodynamic: able to move easily through water

inspired: motivated to come up with a new idea, usually creative

nervous system: the system of body parts that directs electricity in the body to control movement and feeling

noise: random and unwanted electrical signals

pigments: substances that change the color of something

predators: animals that hunt or eat other animals

reefs: ridges of rock, sand, or coral near the surface of the ocean

researchers: people whose job it is to study a topic in great detail

satellite: a man-made object that orbits Earth and is used to send data signals

technology: tools and knowledge used to meet a need or solve a problem

thresholds: the points or levels at which something happen

triggers: causes something to start working

tsunami: a large wave from the ocean that causes destruction when it reaches land

Index

AV2

Get the best of both worlds.

AV2 bridges the gap between print and digital.

The expandable resources toolbar enables quick access to content including **videos**, **audio**, **activities**, **weblinks**, **slideshows**, **quizzes**, and **key words**.

Animated videos make static images come alive.

Resource icons on each page help readers to further **explore key concepts**.

Published by AV2
14 Penn Plaza, 9th Floor New York, NY 10122
Website: www.av2books.com

Copyright ©2021 AV2
All rights reserved. No part of this publication may be reproduced, stored in a retrieval system, or transmitted in any form or by any means, electronic, mechanical, photocopying, recording, or otherwise, without the prior written permission of the publisher.

Library of Congress Cataloging-in-Publication Data

Names: Miller, Tessa, author. | Nixon, Madeline, author.
Title: Inventions inspired by oceanic animals / Tessa Miller and Madeline Nixon.
Description: New York, NY : AV2 [2021] | Series: Technology inspired by animals | Includes bibliographical references and index. | Audience: Ages 11-14. | Audience: Grades 4-6.
Identifiers: LCCN 2019046696 (print) | LCCN 2019046697 (ebook) | ISBN 9781791118204 (library binding) | ISBN 9781791118211 (paperback) | ISBN 9781791118228 (electronic) | ISBN 9781791118235 (electronic)
Subjects: LCSH: Bionics--Juvenile literature. | Biomimicry--Juvenile literature. | Marine animals--Juvenile literature.
Classification: LCC TA164.2 .M55 2021 (print) | LCC TA164.2 (ebook) | DDC 600--dc23
LC record available at https://lccn.loc.gov/2019046696
LC ebook record available at https://lccn.loc.gov/2019046697

Printed in Guangzhou, China
1 2 3 4 5 6 7 8 9 0 24 23 22 21 20

052020
101519

Art Director: Terry Paulhus Project Coordinator: Priyanka Das

Every reasonable effort has been made to trace ownership and to obtain permission to reprint copyright material. The publisher would be pleased to have any errors or omissions brought to its attention so that they may be corrected in subsequent printings.

The publisher acknowledges Getty Images, iStock, Minden, and Shutterstock as its primary image suppliers for this title.

First published by Full Tilt Press in 2019.

View new titles and product videos at www.av2books.com